BUNGALOW BASICS
KITCHENS

By Paul Duchscherer

Photography by Douglas Keister

Pomegranate

SAN FRANCISCO

Published by Pomegranate Communications, Inc.
Box 808022, Petaluma, California 94975
800-227-1428; www.pomegranate.com

Pomegranate Europe Ltd.
Unit 1, Heathcote Business Centre, Hurlbutt Road
Warwick, Warwickshire CV34 6TD, U. K.
44 1926 430111

Library of Congress Cataloging-in-Publication Data
Duchscherer, Paul.
    Bungalow basics. Kitchens / by Paul Duchscherer ; photography by
Douglas Keister.
        p. cm.
    ISBN 0-7649-2776-0
    1. Bungalows–United States. 2. Kitchens–United States. 3. Arts and crafts
movement–United States. I. Title: Kitchens. II. Keister, Douglas. III. Title.

    NA7571.D8225 2004
    728'.373–dc22

                                                    2003062206

Pomegranate Catalog No. A701

Designed by Patrice Morris

Printed in Korea

13 12 11 10 09 08 07 06 05 04   10 9 8 7 6 5 4 3 2 1

This book is dedicated to the discovery,
appreciation, and preservation of bungalows,
and especially to all those who
love and care for them.

Acknowledgments

Because of space limitations, we regret that it is not possible to acknowledge each of those individuals and organizations who have helped us with this book. Our heartfelt appreciation is extended especially to all the homeowners who, by graciously sharing their homes with us, have made this book a reality. Special thanks are given also to Sandy Schweitzer, John Freed, and Don Merrill for their tireless support, unflagging encouragement, and invaluable assistance. We salute you!

At the end of the book, we have noted a few of the talented artisans, architects, designers, craftspeople, and manufacturers whose work appears here, but space constraints preclude us from crediting each one. We offer them all our deepest gratitude. Alternatively, our readers may wish to consult the extensive credit listings in our earlier book series, published by Penguin Putnam Inc. (comprising *The Bungalow: America's Arts & Crafts Home, Inside the Bungalow: America's Arts & Crafts Interior,* and *Outside the Bungalow: America's Arts & Crafts Garden*), which make reference to many of the images that are also included in this book.

Thee bungalow earned its reputation for practical planning largely through the merits of its kitchen. Incorporating technological innovations that were rapidly transforming domestic life, bungalow designers created basic kitchen arrangements that helped reduce the drudgery of daily housekeeping. For as the twentieth century dawned, it became increasingly apparent that nearly every domestic task in most middle-class households would be the sole responsibility of an unassisted housewife.

After 1900, the advertising campaigns of almost every major industry reflected an insistent push toward all things "modern." As the new century's economy expanded, job opportunities increased; consequently, the number of American households in the market for new homes also grew. The younger generation, seeking affordable starter homes, were most receptive to the latest styles and innovations in the housing market. The bungalow's promise of "the simple life" proved to be a powerful lure, and for many fledgling housewives, its kitchen epitomized modernity and convenience.

The introduction of the bungalow coincided with the spread of electric power for residential use. Under development since the late Victorian era, electric service gradually replaced gas as the preferred power source for interior and exterior lighting (although gas was widely used to power home furnaces and water heaters, commonly called "boilers"). As late as the 1920s, in areas where electric service remained less reliable, some bungalows were actually outfitted for both gas and electric lighting. Most kitchen lighting fixtures were strictly utilitarian, designed to deliver a maximum amount of light with a minimum of fuss (Figures 4, 9, 39, 40, 43, 47). Often, the typical central ceiling fixture was augmented by a smaller wall-mounted light above the sink (Figures 7, 9–10).

In addition to transforming how homes were lit, electricity unleashed a demand for "indispensable" plug-in household appliances. Portable electric heaters and vacuums enjoyed a wide popularity. Aimed at a newly servantless middle class, the market for countertop gadgets reflected the public's obsession with convenience and modernity (Figures 11–13).

Accelerating most rapidly in and around cities, the growing demand for reliable electric service fostered development in another way. As once-isolated sections of cities across the country became linked to their downtowns by electric-powered streetcar lines, these areas became viable sites for new housing tracts. With electricity to thank, many bungalow neighborhoods were thus nicknamed "streetcar suburbs."

Earlier bungalow kitchens, like those in the nineteenth century, frequently had a bulky cast-iron stove, powered by wood or coal or possibly both (Figures 1–2). Some were later converted to gas, occasionally retaining the capability of using more than one fuel source.

While electricity eclipsed gas as a power source for lighting in the early twentieth century, it lagged behind when it came to cooking. Stove manufacturers did not immediately embrace electrical technology on a large scale. The popularity of single- and double-burner countertop "hot plates" was an exception, but they were intended mostly for light or occasional use, such as in an efficiency apartment, rented room, or vacation cabin. Although electric ranges had been developed and marketed by the 1920s, they did not come into common use until later decades.

Then as now, many people preferred to cook on gas stoves, and they became standard equipment in many bungalow kitchens. Among the most familiar vintage appliances still in use today are the classic gas stoves with gracefully curving metal legs, most of which date to the 1920s (Figures 14, 17, 24, 26–27). Especially valued are the deluxe, oversized models with additional burners, an extra oven, and possibly a griddle, a plate-warming compartment, and storage drawers (Figures 4, 8–9, 28, 40, 43, 47). Many stoves also had a gas-fired trash-burning compartment. White porcelain enamel finishes were the most prevalent choice for stoves and other appliances, but the 1920s and 1930s saw the introduction of some color. The most popular schemes included combinations of pale cream and soft green, sometimes accented in black. The brisk market for reconditioned vintage appliances today is a testament to their aesthetics, performance, and durability.

Portable electric tabletop fans might have aided interior ventilation, but kitchens had special problems to solve. Just above the stove in many bungalow kitchens, a small, square, screen-covered opening in the ceiling helped exhaust the steam and smoke generated by cooking. Vented through the roof, some openings had a closeable metal door that could be operated by pulling on a chain. This passive ventilation system relied simply on the natural convection of warm air rising; few moving parts (and no power requirement) made it a popular and practical solution. Electric-powered fan venting eventually supplanted the passive system in most homes, but many working examples still survive. The stoves in higher-budget kitchens were often vented through oversized hoods, which better contained the rising heat and smoke (Figures 4, 27–28, 43). Typically made of reinforced plaster and built in place (although some were made entirely of sheet metal), large stove hoods often featured an electric task light inside, to reduce shadowing.

Other than the stove, the most important kitchen appliance was the refrigerator. In earlier bungalow kitchens, these were most likely to be true iceboxes, which relied on the cooling effects of ice blocks inside a metal-lined cabinet. Iceboxes tended to be located on back porches, to facilitate ice deliveries (Figure 22). Melting ice could be drained into drip pans (which required emptying), but a far preferable solution was to have a pipe fitting that drained the water outside the house. A more convenient placement of this appliance within the kitchen proper eventually came with the advent of more efficient electric-powered refrigerators (Figures 14–16).

Many bungalow kitchens had additional food storage in the form of a separate cooler, sometimes called a California cooler because of its typical use in bungalows there. Usually consisting of a tall, narrow cabinet fitted with wire shelves and screened openings, it allowed the cooler air beneath the house to circulate up through the cabinet and out an exterior wall (Figures 7, 10). This passive cooling system was not only inexpensive but also ideal for storing many types of perishable food because it could successfully maintain even temperatures. While many original coolers remain intact and continue to be used, others have been sealed off and survive now only as conventional cabinet storage.

Since most bungalow kitchens did not have enough space to accommodate a freestanding table and chairs, the introduction of the built-in "breakfast nook" proved to be a great, if rather compact, innovation for smaller homes (Figures 20–22, 41). Saving steps and time, it allowed housewives to serve some of the family meals in the kitchen. It also provided a convenient and well-lit place for children to do their homework under a mother's watchful gaze (and within close reach of the cookie jar). Breakfast nooks typically consisted of a narrow table set between two facing benches. Most models had lift-up seats, with storage space below. Some also had hinged, lift-up table-tops that made for easier cleaning and seating access.

The efficiency of a bungalow kitchen's layout often depended upon how well it was outfitted with built-in cabinetry. Like the modular components of breakfast nook units, kitchen cabinets were usually mass-produced and ordered from a catalog, rather than custom-built on-site. The most popular finish for kitchen cabinetry was durable enamel paint in a pale color such as white or cream, commonly believed to be more "hygienic" (Figures 6–7, 9–10, 17); although less typical, cabinets were also available in unpainted wood finishes (Figures 5, 38). In either case, the room's other woodwork usually received a matching finish.

Cabinet manufacturer's catalogs of the period show a variety of familiar forms that included both upper and lower cabinets. Much like today's versions, some upper cabinets featured glass-paneled doors (Figures 4–5, 7). If space permitted, the modular units could be configured to make up a wall of nearly floor-to-ceiling cabinetry (Figures 40, 42). The most typical door style had a framed, flat, recessed panel. Doors and drawer fronts were usually set flush with the surrounding cabinet face, with no recessed toe space (Figures 7, 10). Simple, functional nickel-plated hardware was an early favorite and included several variations of the "bin pull" used for drawers, two-piece cupboard latches (Figure 39), and exposed butterfly hinges for cabinet doors.

Later, glass knobs and handles (in black, white, and a few pale colors) also became popular. Specialized cabinetry included slide-out cutting boards, deep bin drawers (Figure 10), telephone niches, and—one of the most enduringly practical (and most commonly surviving) of all bungalow kitchen innovations—foldout ironing boards (Figure 17).

Although more typical of nineteenth-century kitchens, some freestanding cabinetry persisted into the bungalow era and beyond. Especially popular was the so-called Hoosier cabinet (originally named for its manufacturer in New Castle, Indiana), which came in many sizes and variations (Figures 18–19). Hoosiers included some combination of pull-out drawers, bins for sugar and flour, a built-in flour sifter, slide-out work surface, handy hooks for cups and utensils, plus other space in which to store dishes and cookware. The self-contained efficiency of the Hoosier cabinet made it a microcosm of bungalow kitchen planning at its best.

Plans for bungalow kitchens gave priority to providing adequate air circulation and natural lighting from as many windows as possible. Some kitchens had windows on more than one wall, but most had room for only a double or triple window over the sink, where good lighting was especially needed (Figures 5–7, 9–10). The small back utility porch, which typically adjoined the kitchen, often had extra windows (Figure 13) and could admit additional light through the doorway (Figure 22) or through an interior window located in the wall between the two areas.

In most bungalow kitchens, outside access was through this back utility porch, where the back door usually opened into the rear yard or onto a side driveway. Occasionally the back porch housed an extra toilet (but rarely a full bathroom). Because milk deliveries were typical during the period, it might also have contained an enclosed compartment for receiving new milk bottles and returning empty ones. Another usual amenity was a deep laundry sink, with a sharply angled front face to accept a scrub board. On wet days, the laundry could be hung up to dry on the back porch. Although some families could afford them sooner, the earliest versions of washing machines and dishwashers remained unaffordable luxuries for most middle-class households for many years (Figure 12).

Finishes for earlier bungalow kitchens tended to be more practical than overtly decorative. The most typical materials used for countertops were wood, usually maple or sugar pine (Figure 10), and porcelain tile; occasionally both wood and tile were used for different countertops within the same kitchen. Counters directly adjacent to the sink were usually tiled and sometimes had slightly slanted surfaces to create built-in drainboards (Figures 7, 32). Small hexagonal porcelain tiles (the same type used for flooring) were the most durable countertop choice; a ceramic tile molding, often in black or another contrasting color (Figures 7, 30, 32), generally trimmed the counter's front edge. For counter backsplashes (and sometimes for walls), the white glazed ceramic tile called subway tile (usually three by six inches, set in a bricklike "running bond" pattern) was a popular choice during much of the period (Figures 1, 4, 6, 10, 27).

Large porcelain-finished cast-iron sinks (usually white) were common. More expensive models had integral drainboards on one or both sides (Figure 3); some also had integral backsplashes (Figures 10, 22). Heavy sinks required strong support; to remain open below for easier cleaning, some were wall-hung (Figure 26), while others rested on matching iron legs (Figure 9) or on enclosed cabinetry bases (Figure 10). In the 1920s, some porcelain sinks and especially ceramic tiles began to appear in colorful glazes (Figures 7, 19, 28–29, 32, 37), although kitchens did not get quite as colorful as bathrooms of that time.

Kitchen flooring materials used throughout the era included hardwood flooring, most typically of oak but sometimes of maple (Figures 4, 9). If hardwood exceeded the budget, softwood (like fir) was commonly used, either stained or painted; some softwood floors were overlaid with a patterned linoleum "rug." Linoleum was an early-twentieth-century kitchen-floor mainstay. Less expensive varieties of linoleum came in solid colors, but intricate patterns—inlaid either at the factory or on-site—were also available (Figures 22–24, 28–29). Occasionally linoleum was also enlisted as a surface for countertops. Cork tile flooring, although less durable and fairly expensive, appealed to some because of its added cushioning effect. Also on the costlier side (but the most durable of all) was unglazed porcelain floor tile. Small, white hexagonal tiles were generally used, with perhaps a few color accents (Figure 10).

As the room where the housewife was destined to spend most of her working hours, the bungalow kitchen received a growing amount of attention to its appearance. The increasing use of color, while slow to take hold, reflected the kitchen's transition from an austere, mostly utilitarian space to a stylishly cozy, cheerful setting for both the rituals of housework and informal family gatherings (Figures 1, 22, 24). Even if most built-in cabinetry and appliances were finished in a "hygienic" white, colored paint was often applied to the walls to add interest. Prior to painting, the plaster of some lower wall areas was scored while still wet to resemble the grout lines of tile. Another treatment for lower wall areas was a wainscot created from vertical, interlocking beadboard (or tongue-in-groove) panels, which were usually painted.

Any wallpapers used in the kitchen were likely to be so-called sanitary papers; with a glossy finish, intended to be varnished for greater moisture resistance, most came in designs that resembled ceramic tile patterns. Stenciling could add a more personal touch of color and pattern, most often in narrow borders around the ceiling but sometimes also on top of wainscoting (Figure 26) or on the faces of cabinet doors. In the 1920s and later, the use of decorative decals in whimsical kitchen motifs was another popular way to adorn cabinet and appliance doors. Throw rugs, patterned curtains, and displays of potted plants or favorite knickknacks could lend even more personality to the room (Figures 1, 5, 19, 22, 24).

Whether original in shape or reconfigured, bungalow kitchens have many stories to tell. Each one has helped pave the way for the kitchen to become the center of family activity today. Studying the scale and features of surviving bungalow kitchens provides valuable lessons in practicality and good design. The following pages offer some excellent examples, both for those interested in re-creating an authentic early-twentieth-century design and those seeking a contemporary interpretation of a period-style kitchen.

1. A rack of decorative china and a warm wall color above the white tile wainscot signal this extra-spacious kitchen's departure from the utilitarian decor of the nineteenth century. Behind the oversized cast-iron stove is a fully tiled wall and below it, a tile floor with a patterned inset; a bordered rug softens the floor. Open space below the sink and other work surfaces made cleaning easier. Built-in upper cabinetry is partially seen at left.

♨ 2 & 3. These kitchen illustrations appeared in the article "A Convenient and Well-equipped Kitchen That Simplifies the Housework," published in the September 1905 issue of Gustav Stickley's magazine, *The Craftsman*. The article proposed that modern kitchens should blend order and efficiency with cheerful, homey comfort; it presented this example as appropriate for either the house-wife or the "servant maid" (although the latter was becoming less common with the growing trend away from hired help).

4. The kitchen in the 1908 Gamble House in Pasadena, California, has a level of quality in its finishes and detailing that architects (and brothers) Charles and Henry Greene lavished on the rest of this famous home (now open to the public). Practical ceramic tile walls set off the maple flooring and cabinetry. The center work table has "through-drawers," which open at either side. Although large, the circa-1930 stove is dwarfed by the original plaster hood.

🔥 5. In a common arrangement, upper cabinets with glass doors and lower cabinets with drawers and cupboards frame a pair of windows and the kitchen sink. From a period catalog of the Morgan Company (which manufactured many other built-ins), this kitchen's unpainted, stained wood cabinets were less typical of the time.

🔥 6. Another vintage catalog presents white painted upper and lower cabinets around the kitchen sink and windows. A cupboard latch secures each door. While the backsplash tile is typical, the floor's bordered treatment (possibly a faux-tile linoleum pattern) is unusually complex. Under the sink, a swing-out stool has an adjustable-height, swiveling seat.

🔥 7. (right) With all its original cabinetry (including a California cooler in the far right corner), this 1909 kitchen remains entirely functional. The baker's table serves as a period-style work island. Vinyl flooring re-creates a popular early linoleum pattern; the backsplash and counter tile most likely date from the 1920s. Over the sink is an original sconce. Not as utilitarian, the art-glass ceiling fixture is more suited to a dining room.

BUNGALOW BASICS

8. In nearly original condition, the kitchen of the 1907 Evans House in Marin County, California (designed by noted local architect Louis C. Mullgardt), has a redwood-paneled ceiling and walls, with a recessed cabinet in the corner. Out of view (to the right) is a walk-through, cabinet-lined pantry. The large 1920s gas range vents through the chimney of the living room fireplace. Within easy reach of the stove is a baker's table. Period-style pendant lights of ribbed glass have supplanted the original single-bulb fixture. The vinyl checkerboard floor has replaced linoleum in a similar pattern.

9. Above the large cast-iron sink supported by matching legs, three casement windows provide good natural lighting and ventilation for this narrow, restored 1911 kitchen. A pair of sconces and ribbed glass pendant lights are recent additions. Between the sink and the period range, a cabinet door (which matches the others) hides a new dishwasher. Cabinets at right frame a doorway to the back porch.

10. The 1915 Lanterman House, an "oversized" bungalow in La Cañada-Flintridge, California (now a house museum), boasts original furnishings and finishes throughout. The butler's pantry, shown here, resembles smaller kitchens of this date, with many typical period features: large cast-iron sink with integral drainboards, subway-tile backsplash, porcelain tile floor, wood countertops, and cabinetry that includes a California cooler (at left), pull-out cutting board, and bin drawer.

🌸 11. *(above, left)* From a 1917 book entitled *Home Interiors,* this illustration shows some of the electric-powered household gadgets (manufactured by Westinghouse) that were fast becoming "essential" for the modern kitchen (left to right, from top): a tea samovar, nursery milk warmer, frying pan, "toaster-stove," coffee percolator, chafing dish, table fan, small power motor ("will run any machine in the house"), sewing machine, and general utility motor (with "a dozen different uses").

🌸 12. *(above, right)* An article on "Kitchen Efficiency" in a 1923 edition of *The Home* touted this built-in electric dishwasher as *de rigueur,* but such things were too pricey for most households. With its swing-arm faucet, soap dish, and integral backsplash and drainboard, it seems more akin to the kitchen sink than an ancestor of today's electric dishwashers.

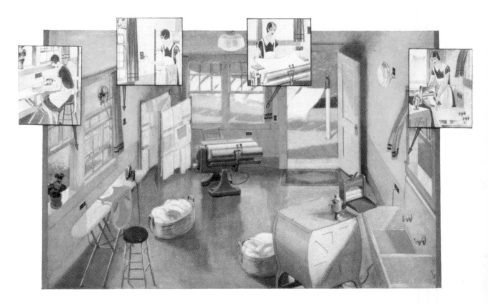

13. Taken from a General Electric advertisement in the April 1929 issue of *Art & Decoration* magazine, this illustration has four small, overlaid images that show a woman in a white apron busily engaged in various household tasks, made easier by electric-powered appliances. Highlighted by downward-pointing arrows, the appliances that correspond to each task appear in the utility porch below; they include a clothes iron, an electric exhaust fan, a mangle (which presses laundry with heated rollers), and a washing machine.

🌹 14. Reconditioned vintage appliances can be a viable option for those seeking the most authentic period-style kitchen possible. In this 1919 kitchen, a compact-sized gas range from the mid-1920s sits next to a 1933 General Electric "Monitor Top" refrigerator. The corner cabinet at right once housed the original narrow-diameter water heater.

15. A General Electric advertisement presented "the first all-steel refrigerator," describing it as "a new small-family model at the very low price of $215" (a princely sum for many households in 1930). Called the Monitor Top for the distinctively visible placement of its cooling coils, it was very popular for small kitchens because of its compact size.

16. Among the most revolutionary early-twentieth-century advances in kitchen technology, electric refrigeration became an indispensable convenience for most families after 1930. Manufacturers constantly updated and streamlined their designs to better fit contemporary kitchens; this model's clean lines helped it blend in with the cabinetry.

🔥 17. This "built-in ironing board outfit" was a popular offering from Sears, Roebuck and Company; this illustration is from a 1926 catalog of the company's "Honor Bilt" homes, which offered different cabinetry options. As early as 1909, Sears shipped such "kit houses" to building sites, where they were then usually constructed by a local builder.

18. Especially for smaller kitchens, the freestanding, multipurpose "Hoosier" cabinet was a popular way to augment the limited storage capacity of built-in cabinetry (even if insufficient space meant placement on the back porch). Associated with baking tasks, the cabinet derived its name from its maker, the Hoosier Manufacturing Company of New Castle, Indiana. This view of a 1917 model shows the Hoosier's typical features and equipment.

19. Compare this Hoosier cabinet (taken from a 1922 magazine advertisement) to the previous example; in its overall form, and most likely in its interior features, it has not changed significantly in five years, but now its wood is painted and its styling simplified. It more closely resembles the typical kitchen cabinets with which it would share space.

🌹 20. From a 1920s catalog of built-in cabinetry, this extra-large breakfast nook displays a whimsical Oriental influence in the forms and cutout shapes of its end panels. The image of two well-dressed ladies having a visit amidst tastefully decorated surroundings was calculatedly appealing to housewives.

🌹 21. From a 1926 Sears catalog (of mostly house plans), this breakfast nook shows a Craftsman influence in the pegged-tenon detailing of its benches and table. The influence of the Colonial Revival style, then becoming more popular, is apparent in the curvaceous outline of the end panels.

🌸 22. A gas range, steaming teakettle, inviting breakfast nook, back-porch icebox, ample cast-iron sink, and cheerful color scheme evoke the quintessential bungalow kitchen. The scene illustrates a linoleum flooring treatment in a 1924 booklet called *Floors, Furniture and Color,* published by the manufacturer Armstrong. Appearing deceptively large, the breakfast nook resembles that in Figure 21.

23. Irregular and random in effect, this 1920s linoleum floor pattern—which survived only in a closet—was meant to suggest old paving stones, perhaps of tile or slate. It has the intentionally "quaint" character that was gaining public favor for home design during that decade. Such "storybook-style" effects also appeared in bungalow architecture.

24. An image from a 1927 linoleum advertisement shows how the taste for more color and historical novelty in decorating (as seen in the last example) might be applied to an entire kitchen. Colonial Revival-style furnishings are reflected in the "antique tile" floor, alongside a modern gas stove tucked behind a cabinet door's painted folk art.

BUNGALOW BASICS

25. With original fir flooring and native redwood walls and ceiling, this kitchen was remodeled to include new matching cabinetry and a wood-clad vent hood. The house was built in Marin County, California, in 1904 for C. Hart Merriam, a noted anthropologist and naturalist. Sufficiently roomy for a table and chairs, the kitchen is a blend of old and new. Striking grids of deep blue tiles accent work areas.

26. This corner vignette from a 1920s magazine ad features some familiar kitchen forms of the period. A two-tone gas range, set on curving cabriole legs, is embellished with the Dutch Cleanser logo (a little Dutch girl, who "chases dirt") on its oven and broiler doors. This motif cleverly recurs in the flooring pattern and as a border atop the wainscot. Open below, the wall-hung cast-iron sink allows easier dirt chasing.

27. Although not apparent from the looks of its tidy original kitchen, the 1927 home built by William S. Hart (a famous silent-film star of Westerns) on his ranch in Newhall, California, is an example of the Spanish Colonial Revival style. Called "La Loma de los Vientos," the house is open to the public as a museum. A practical but costly (and hence uncommon) detail is the tiled interior of the outsized vent hood for a classic gas range.

28. In another Spanish Colonial Revival house, this kitchen's colorfully tiled countertop and backsplash areas show the influence of the home's exterior. A striking inlaid linoleum floor is a notable exception to the kitchen's otherwise typical period features (e.g., cabinet style, gas range, and large hood). "Casa Nueva" was completed for Walter P. Temple in 1927; it is now open to the public as part of the Workman and Temple Family Homestead Museum, in City of Industry, California.

29. The butler's pantry of Casa Nueva (partially visible between the two doorways in Figure 28) adjoins the kitchen. It includes a built-in lower cabinet with an integral sink and a countertop of "nickel silver" (a forerunner of stainless steel), which was easy to keep clean. Vivid checkerboard tile accents the backsplash and windowsill. Exaggerated by a pair of angled side cabinets, the outer wall's thickness recalls that of adobe construction.

🌺 30. *(left)* This kitchen's countertop was recently installed using period-appropriate white hexagonal porcelain tile and blue-green glazed ceramic edging. Set in a grid rather than the typical "running bond" pattern, the white subway tile of the backsplash (two by four inches) is also smaller than usual; a narrow blue-green tile accent band runs across it.

🌺 31. *(left, bottom)* A recently installed backsplash incorporates accents of period Art Nouveau tiles from England, which have inspired the color scheme for the new glazed tiles that now surround them. Set directly below the accent tiles, a narrow maroon border helps integrate them into the background field of apple green subway tiles.

🌺 32. The backsplash tile and accent banding in this 1920s kitchen are original, but made to match is the custom-colored tile used for the edging and inset borders of the new white tile countertop. Gently sloping built-in drainboards on either side of the original sink are a period touch. The tile's color scheme is repeated in the cabinet paint color.

33. Retaining much of its original character in keeping with the home's Spanish Colonial Revival style, this kitchen features hand-forged iron hardware on its rustic wooden cabinetry. Terra-cotta pavers are used throughout, with matching tile on the countertops. Behind the stove, a new hand-painted tile panel adjoins a simpler tile back-splash; the plaster-encased vent hood is an appropriate new addition. The 1933 Roper House in San Diego, California, was designed by noted architect Cliff May, best known as an early pioneer in the development of post-World War II American ranch houses.

🌸 34 & 35. In 1930, prominent local architect Douglas Ellington completed his own home in Asheville, North Carolina, using diverse building materials recycled from his various project construction sites. The kitchen reflects the home's picturesque, handmade feel. In lieu of much built-in cabinetry, it utilizes freestanding wood furnishings. Atop buff-colored brick walls, a frieze pattern of contrasting brick encircles the room. In the detail view above, an arched brick recess that houses the stove has a venting fan concealed behind handcrafted wooden doors.

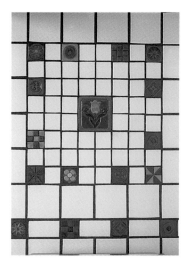

36. Recently set into the backsplash behind a stove, this accent panel combines colorful handmade tiles with plain white field tiles of a matching size, set within a grid of larger white field tiles (which cover the remaining backsplash areas). Below, interspersed accent tiles create a border that extends to adjoining areas.

37. Well known as designers and builders of atmospheric Spanish Colonial Revival "courtyard" apartment housing in the Los Angeles area, Arthur and Nina Zwebell built their finest project, "The Andalusia," in West Hollywood in 1926. One large unit became their home. Here, simple (but appropriate) detailing in their kitchen includes handwrought iron hardware, a terra-cotta tile floor, hand-painted accent tiles and base trim, herringbone-patterned tile counters and backsplash, and a corbeled wooden beam spanning the windows. An arched opening under the sink makes cleaning easier.

🐿 38. The wooden cabinets are original in this 1911 kitchen, but the tile flooring and countertops date from a recent remodel, which also included the addition of a dishwasher, set behind a matching wood panel. A small, separate breakfast room, glimpsed through the door at right, was a bonus feature of some bungalow plans.

39. In an early-twentieth-century Craftsman-style home, this kitchen was re-created with an eye toward the straightforward, utilitarian character it had lost through insensitive remodeling. Period-style hardware and painted cabinetry blend with white glazed tile counters and backsplash; the tile extends to full height in the stove alcove. A vintage stove and refrigerator from the post-World War II era lend character.

40. Because the original kitchen of the 1911 Keyes bungalow in Altadena, California (on the National Register of Historic Places), had already been lost to remodelings, the bungalow's current owners took design cues from the Gamble House kitchen (Figure 4), incorporating similar woodwork, ceramic tiled walls, and utilitarian pendant lighting into their new kitchen. A separate dining table provides extra work space, and a wall of full-height cabinetry (at left) offers generous storage. On the opposite wall (out of view) is the sink, under a row of windows.

🌹 41 & 42. In a 1914 Prairie-style home in Seattle, a recent remodel replaced an earlier inappropriate kitchen. The original kitchen was well-documented in plans and photographs that accompanied a 1916 cover-story article about the house in *Bungalow Magazine,* which provided inspiration and guidance for this version. In Figure 42 (right), the distinctive geometric divisions in the upper cabinets' glass doors replicate a signature detail of Ellsworth Storey, the noted architect who designed this home. A skylight was added, and new appliances were incorporated into a wall of floor-to-ceiling cabinets at left. In Figure 41, the sink wall's original windows also have the geometric divisions favored by Storey. Offset by the traditional warmth of hardwood flooring, granite countertops lend a modern touch. For better access, the tabletop of a compact breakfast nook slides in and out. A deep storage drawer in the built-in bench at right keeps children's art supplies handy.

43. Once a chopped-up space that included a kitchen, pantry, maid's room, and bath, this spacious new kitchen was made possible by combining those areas in a recent remodel. A reconfigured separate pantry provides a second sink and an extra dishwasher. An enormous vintage gas range, found by the owners during the remodel, is now comfortably accommodated. Hardwood floors, period-style cabinetry, "schoolhouse" lighting fixtures, and a large plaster-faced vent hood (inspired by earlier models) all add charm and utility. The central "island" is a freestanding cabinet.

44 & 45. After weighing the options, the owners of a vintage bungalow decided that the only way to make their existing kitchen feel bigger was to add more space, but they did not want to change the home's exterior look, and their budget was tight. Their solution was to remove a wall and doorway that separated the kitchen from a small breakfast room (at the far end) and combine the two areas. In Figure 45 (right), the counter space on the left has been extended, allowing room for new appliances. To enhance the feeling of spaciousness, the owners avoided using upper cabinets in most of the room and installed open shelving (Figure 44) instead. Helping to unify the room are new linoleum flooring and a high display shelf.

46. In a recent bungalow remodel, the efficient U-shaped layout of the original kitchen was retained, but the wall that separated it from a small breakfast room (in the foreground) was removed. This alteration greatly expanded the feeling of space and improved the sight lines, allowing for better visibility of the fine period lighting, a striking new handmade copper hood, and new quartersawn oak cabinets with handcrafted copper hardware. A simple tile backsplash, inset with period tiles, is paired with marble countertops. Suspended from open Prairie-style supports, an upper cabinet (at center) has glass doors on both sides for more light. Arts and Crafts textiles contribute interesting pattern and color. Providing direct garden access, French doors (at left) lead to a small deck along one side of the house.

47. This kitchen in a 1905 Craftsman-style home was remodeled to create the appearance of a period kitchen while retaining all the modern conveniences. It has succeeded admirably, with the cabinetry at left containing a refrigerator (disguised by wooden panels) and a microwave oven (behind a flip-up door) to the left of the vintage stove. With a maple butcher-block top, the center island houses a hidden dishwasher, which faces toward the sink.

Used in an architectural journal, it described a single-story, shingled Cape Cod summerhouse ringed by covered porches. By the 1900s, *bungalow* had become part of our popular vocabulary, at first associated with vacation homes, both seaside and mountain. The bungalow's informality, a refreshing contrast to stuffy Victorian houses, helped fuel its popularity as a year-round home. It had its greatest fame as a modest middle-class house from 1900 to 1930.

Widely promoted, the bungalow was touted for its modernity, practicality, affordability, convenience, and often-artistic design. Expanding industry and a favorable economy across the country created an urgent need for new, affordable, middle-class housing, which the bungalow was just in time to meet.

In America, a bungalow implied a basic plan, rather than a specific style, of modest house. Typically, it consisted of 1,200 to 1,500 square feet, with living room, dining room, kitchen, two bedrooms, and bathroom all on one level. Some bungalows had roomy attic quarters, but most attics were bare or intended to be developed as the family's needs grew. A bungalow set in a garden fulfilled many Americans' dream of a home of their own.

Widely publicized California bungalows in the early 1900s spawned frenzied construction in booming urban areas across the country. In design, most bungalows built prior to World War I adopted the so-called Craftsman style, sometimes combined with influences from the Orient, the Swiss chalet, or the Prairie style. After the war, public taste shifted toward historic housing styles, and bungalows adapted Colonial Revival, English cottage, Tudor, Mission, and Spanish Colonial Revival features.

Today Craftsman is the style most associated with bungalows. Characterized inside and out by use of simple horizontal lines, Craftsman style relies on the artistry of exposed wood joinery (often visible on front porch detailing). Natural or rustic materials (wood siding, shingles, stone, and clinker brick) are favored. Interiors may be enriched with beamed ceilings, high wainscot paneling, art glass, and hammered copper or metalwork lighting accents.

The word *Craftsman* was coined by prominent furniture manufacturer and tastemaker Gustav Stickley, who used it to label his line of sturdy, slat-backed furniture (also widely known as Mission style), which was influenced by the English Arts and Crafts movement. That movement developed in the mid-nineteenth century as a reaction against the Industrial Revolution. Early leaders such as John Ruskin and William Morris turned to the medieval past for inspiration as they sought to preserve craft skills disappearing in the wake of factory mechanization.

In both the decorative arts (furniture, wallpaper, textiles, glass, metalwork, and ceramics) and architecture, the Arts and Crafts movement advocated use of the finest natural materials to make practical and beautiful designs, executed with skillful handcraftsmanship. One goal was to improve the poor-quality, mass-produced home furnishings available to the rising middle class. Morris and a group of like-minded friends founded a business to produce well-designed, handcrafted goods for domestic interiors. Although the company aspired to make its goods affordable to all, it faced the inevitable conflict between quality and cost. However, its Arts and Crafts example inspired many others in England (and eventually in America) to relearn treasured old craft traditions and continue them for posterity.

As it grew, the movement also became involved in politics, pressing for social reforms. Factory workers trapped in dull, repetitive jobs (with little hope for anything better) were among their chief concerns; they saw the workers' fate as a waste of human potential and talent.

The idealistic and visionary English movement's artistic goals of design reform were more successful than its forays into social reform. Perhaps its greatest success, in both England and the United States, was in giving the public a renewed sense of the value of quality materials, fine craftsmanship, and good design in times of rapid world change.

The Arts and Crafts movement had multiple influences on the American bungalow. The movement arrived here from England in the early 1900s, just as the bungalow was becoming popular. Among its most successful promoters was Elbert Hubbard, founder of the Roycroft Community, a group of artisans producing handmade books and decorative arts inspired by Morris. Hubbard also published two periodicals and sold goods by mail order.

Gustav Stickley was another American inspired by England's important reform movement and soon was expressing this inspiration in the sometimes austere but well-made designs of his Craftsman style. Becoming an influential promoter of the bungalow as an ideal "Craftsman home," he marketed furniture, lighting, metalwork, and textiles styled appropriately for it. His magazine, *The Craftsman,* was a popular vehicle for his ideas and products, and he sold plans for the Craftsman houses he published in his magazine. The wide popularity of his Craftsman style spread the aesthetic sensibilities of the Arts and Crafts movement into countless American middle-class households, making it a growing influence on architecture and decorative arts here. (England in the early twentieth century remarkably had no middle-class housing form comparable to the American bungalow, but Australia has bungalows of that period, inspired by ours, rather than any from Britain.)

Other manufacturers eventually contributed to Stickley's downfall by blatantly copying his ideas and products and eroding his market share. Once Stickley's exclusive brand name, the word *Craftsman* was assimilated into general use and became public property after his bankruptcy in 1916.

Americans choosing the Craftsman style for their homes, interiors, and furnishings rarely were committed to the artistic and philosophical reforms of the Arts and Crafts movement; most were simply following a vogue. Prospective homeowners (and real estate developers) usually selected their bungalow designs from inexpensive sets of plans marketed in catalogs called plan books; few used an architect's services. Some people even bought prefabricated "ready-cut" or "kit" houses. First sold in 1909 by Sears, Roebuck and Company, prefabricated houses soon were widely copied. In the heat of bungalow mania, Sears and others offered tempting incentives to prospective bungalow buyers, such as bonus financing for their lots. For a time, it was said that if you had a job, you could afford a bungalow. But when jobs were in short supply as the Great Depression hit, many defaulted on their little dream homes, leaving their creditors stung.

The depression ended the heyday of the bungalow, but its practical innovations reappeared in later houses, then more likely to be called cottages. The post-World War II ranch house could be considered the legacy of the bungalow. Only recently has a rising demand for lower-cost houses triggered a reevaluation of vintage bungalow stock as viable housing. In response to public demand, the home planning and construction industries have reprised some of the obvious charms of the bungalow in new homes. A real boon for homeowners seeking to restore or renovate a vintage bungalow (or perhaps build a new one) is today's flourishing Arts and Crafts revival, fueled by the demand for a wide array of newly crafted home furnishings that reflect the traditions and spirit of the Arts and Crafts movement. 🔨

CREDITS

Figure 9: Restoration architect: Martin Eli Weil. **Figure 25:** Light boxes by Nowell's; tile by Heath Ceramics; **Figure 32:** Countertop tile by Pratt and Larson; sink hardware by Chicago Faucet. **Figure 36:** Tile by Pratt and Larson. **Figure 38:** Restoration contractor: Elder Vides. **Figure 39:** Renovation architect: James D. McCord. **Figures 41–42:** Renovation architect: Joseph W. Greif. **Figure 43:** Renovation architect: Timothy Anderson; curtains by Dianne Ayres, Arts & Crafts Period Textiles. **Figure 46:** General contractor: Marshall White Construction; cabinetry by Mike Marnell; period lighting from Ron Collier; window coverings and table linens by Dianne Ayres, Arts & Crafts Period Textiles; backsplash field tile by Tile Restoration Center; copper hood by Lowell Chaput; hardware by Buffalo Studios; china coffee service (on center countertop) from Roycroft Shops, Inc. **Figure 49:** General contractor: Shawn Gabel; interior design: Colleen Monahan and homeowner; lighting by Arroyo Craftsman; hardware by Chris Efker, Craftsman Hardware. **Figure 50:** Renovation architect: Glen Jarvis, Jarvis Architects; ceiling light by Arroyo Craftsman.

ARCHIVAL IMAGES

Figures 1, 5, 11, 18, 20, 22: Courtesy the collection of Dianne Ayres and Timothy Hansen, Arts & Crafts Period Textiles. **Figures 2–3, 6, 17, 21:** Courtesy of Dover Publications, Inc. **Figures 13, 15–16:** From the collection of Douglas Keister. **Figures 12, 19, 24, 26:** From the collection of Paul Duchscherer.